The COMPANIONS

Network

www.companionsinchrist.org

M

So much more!

Companions in Christ is *so much more* than printed resources.
It offers an ongoing LEADERSHIP NETWORK that provides:
- Opportunities to connect with other small groups who are also journeying through the *Companions in Christ* series
- Insights and testimonies from other *Companions in Christ* participants
- An online discussion room where you can share or gather information
- Training opportunities that develop and deepen the leadership skills used in formational groups
- Helpful leadership tips and articles as well as updated lists of supplemental resources
- A staff available to consult with you to meet the needs of your small group

Just complete this card and drop it in the mail, and you can enjoy the many benefits available through the *Companions in Christ* NETWORK!

Name: _____

Address: _____

City/State/Zip: _____

Church: _____

Email: _____ Phone: _____

ETWPB

MAIL TO: COMPANIONS *in Christ*

UPPER ROOM MINISTRIES
PO BOX 340012
NASHVILLE, TN 37203-9540

The Companions in Christ Series

EXPLORING
the Way

An Introduction to the Spiritual Journey

PARTICIPANT'S BOOK

Marjorie J. Thompson

UPPER
ROOM BOOKS®
NASHVILLE

COMPANIONS IN CHRIST
EXPLORING THE WAY: AN INTRODUCTION TO THE SPIRITUAL JOURNEY
Participant's Book
Copyright © 2005 by Upper Room Books®
All rights reserved.

The Upper Room® Web site http://www.upperroom.org

Page 88 constitutes an extension of this copyright page.

Cover design: Lori Putnam
Cover art: Lori Putnam
Interior icon development: Michael C. McGuire, SettingPace
Second printing: 2005

Library of Congress Cataloging-in-Publication

Thompson, Marjorie J., 1953–
      Exploring the way: an introduction to the spiritual journey: participant's book.
            p. cm.
Includes bibliographical references.
      ISBN 0-8358-9806-7
      1. Spiritual life—Christianity. 2. Spiritual formation. I. Title.
BV4501.3.T474 2005
248.4—dc22   2004029917

Printed in the United States of America

For more information on *Companions in Christ*
call 800-972-0433 or visit www.companionsinchrist.org

Contents

Acknowledgments   5

Introduction   7

Week 1   Beginning the Journey   11

Week 2   Sharing the Adventure   21

Week 3   Bread for the Journey   31

Week 4   Drink for the Journey   39

Week 5   Companions on the Way   49

Week 6   Reaching Out in Love   57

Glossary of Terms in Spirituality   67

Just the FAQs: Frequently Asked Questions   72

An Annotated Resource List   73

Notes   83

Sources and Authors of Quotes for Further Reflection   85

About the Author   87

Journal   89

Acknowledgments

The original twenty-eight-week *Companions in Christ* resource grew from the seeds of a vision long held by Stephen D. Bryant, editor and publisher of Upper Room Ministries. It was given shape by Marjorie J. Thompson, director of the Pathways Center for Congregational Spirituality, which houses the Companions in Christ initiative of Upper Room Ministries. The vision, which has now expanded into the Companions in Christ series, was realized through the efforts of many people over many years. The original advisers, consultants, authors, editors, and test churches are acknowledged in the foundational twenty-eight-week resource, as well as in the second title of the series, *Companions in Christ: The Way of Forgiveness*. We continue to owe an immense debt of gratitude to each person and congregation there named.

Exploring the Way: An Introduction to the Spiritual Journey is the fifth title in the Companions in Christ series and is intended to be both a bridge resource to the twenty-eight-week resource and a stand-alone resource. The development of *Exploring the Way* is in direct response to the needs expressed by churches and groups around the country for a brief introductory Companions resource that churches can use again and again to orient their members to the spiritual life and to increase participation in spiritual-formation groups in their church.

The progression for the six-week journey through *Exploring the Way* and the writing of the spiritual exercises and compiling of articles found in the Participant's Book are the work of Marjorie Thompson. Marjorie Thompson and Stephen Bryant wrote the material in the Leader's Guide. A staff advisory team comprised of Marjorie Thompson, Stephen Bryant,

Cindy Helms, Robin Pippin, and Tony Peterson contributed to the development of this resource. In addition, Companions trainers and others offered valuable insight and guidance for developing *Exploring the Way*. This group included Eileen Campbell-Reed, Schuyler Bissell, Carol Brown, Doris A. Miller, Frank Granger, Carolyn Shapard, Judy Prather, Bo Prosser, Lynn Dyke, Barbara Cavalluzzi, Tim Goss, Jorene Swift, Sarah Bentley, Evie Waack, Drew Henderson, Zora Rockney, David Bowen, Taylor Mills, and Gail Burns.

A group of Companions trainers led test groups in their congregations or ministry settings that have offered valuable insight and guidance for developing *Exploring the Way*. The trainers and congregations represented by the groups include the following: Beth Link McConnell, Providence Baptist Church, Charlotte, NC; Lisa Gray-Lion, Chelsea First United Methodist Church, Chelsea, MI; Mary Jayne Allen, First Baptist Church of Chattanooga, Chattanooga, TN; Devita Parnell, Highland Hills Baptist Church, Macon, GA.

Introduction

> *You have created us for yourself,*
> *And our hearts are restless until they rest in you.*
> —SAINT AUGUSTINE, *4th century*

With these words Augustine of Hippo, one of the great theologians of the early church, expressed our human hunger for communion with God. We are a restless species, never fully satisfied with life as it is. We long for more than what the world presents on the surface. As human beings, we search for meaning, purpose, a sense of destiny. We yearn for love, genuine acceptance, and a deep sense of belonging. And we want to make a difference for good in this world, to be part of what God is about in redeeming and healing a fallen humanity and a wounded creation.

God made us for this search. We are all trying to find our way back to our spiritual home, back to the Love that gave us life. We cannot fully rest until we come to the place of our soul's origin. This journey homeward to God is known as "the spiritual journey." But how shall we undertake it? What is the path, and where are the markers along the way? With whom do we travel, and do we have an experienced guide?

Many anxious questions can rise in our minds as we ponder moving closer to God. We may feel unsure about traveling this road with the person who stands next to us. We may not be certain that we want to go down this road at all. What if God makes demands of us along the way, and we don't feel prepared? The idea of drawing closer to God is not always a comforting thought.

You are not alone in your thoughts, feelings, or questions. All of us know at times the experience of yearning for God and at other times the sense of feeling repelled from

God. We need one another to support our common seeking and to share gathered wisdom that speaks to our fears. We are not meant to walk the path toward God alone.

The resource you hold in your hands is an introduction to the Christian spiritual life for use in a group setting. If you have ever wondered what the spiritual journey is about or wished you understood better the language of spirituality, this resource is for you. If you have ever desired to be part of a small group that explores questions and issues of faith but felt anxious about the dynamics of small groups or simply too busy to commit to a long-term study, this resource is for you. It will work just as well with a larger class as with a smaller group and only commits you to six weeks of exploration plus a preparatory meeting.

Exploring the Way will introduce you to basic concepts in the Christian spiritual life, along with biblical texts that undergird them. Stories and illustrations in each chapter will help you connect these basic concepts with your daily experience. To help orient you, the resource offers definitions of terms frequently used to describe the spiritual journey. Most importantly, you will begin to learn spiritual practices (disciplines) that can sustain you on the journey: scriptural meditation, prayer, daily examen, listening, and journaling. There is nothing complicated about these practices. They are easily learned and may prove deeply satisfying to you. You will have a chance to "taste and see" one discipline each week in your meeting time and to reflect with others on your experience with the practice. Further opportunity for practice comes during the week as you use the spiritual exercises between meetings.

Each meeting will begin with a brief time of centering and worship, which might consist of a song and a prayer or the lighting of a candle and the reading of a Bible passage that sets the stage for the week's theme. You will also have an opportunity to share about the previous week's spiritual practice and your experience with the spiritual exercises you did during the week.

Your leader will then present information about the week's theme, "setting the stage" for the spiritual practice you will consider. You will have a chance to interact with these ideas and with other participants in the meeting.

Then you will be invited to "taste test" the spiritual discipline for the week, followed by the sharing of questions, insights, and perhaps further information to further aid your understanding of this practice.

The meeting closes with a brief time of prayer and song.

Each session becomes more meaningful if you read the material in this Participant's Book and try a few of the spiritual exercises each week. Just as you cannot learn to play an instrument or a sport without practice, so you cannot learn spiritual disciplines without practice. No one expects you to become a skilled player in just six weeks! But perhaps, as you are introduced to spiritual disciplines over these six weeks, you will begin to sense your own hunger for a closer walk with God in this world. If you catch the "wind of grace" and feel the tug of the Spirit upon you, other resources can take you farther on the journey and other people can accompany you.

We hope that *Exploring the Way* will serve as a bridge to the foundation resource, *Companions in Christ*, a twenty-eight-week program that offers a core understanding of the basics of spiritual formation through personal study, reflection, and small-group process. It explores in depth the Christian spiritual life under five headings: Journey, Scripture, Prayer, Call, and Spiritual Guidance. Since groups may take a break between each of the five parts, members commit only to five or six weeks at a time and determine together when to resume each part.

You may decide that another resource would better serve to help you take the next step in your spiritual growth. The Annotated Resource List in the back of this Participant's Book highlights appropriate book studies.

So put on your walking shoes, set your sights on the path ahead, and prepare to enjoy the adventure God places before you! In *Exploring the Way*, may you find a way of grace, joy, and peace—the way of Christ himself, who accompanies us all.

That is what Christianity is all about—
becoming lovers. The mission of the Church
is just loving people. And our confession?
What is our confession? It is that we do not
know how to love. Until we have made that
confession, there is nothing to be learned.
We cannot even be a beginner with the beginners, and in the School of Christianity there
is nothing else to be but a beginner. [1]

—Elizabeth O'Connor

Week 1

Beginning the Journey

*We do not want to be beginners. But let us be convinced of the fact
that we will never be anything else but beginners, all our life![2]*
—THOMAS MERTON, *Contemplative Prayer*

Setting the Stage

1. Life is a journey from "womb to tomb."

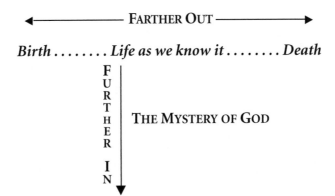

2. Life is a sacred journey encompassed by the mystery of God.

   Extending "farther out"—the journey of life extends in both directions beyond what
   we know

Extending "further in"—the journey also extends to meaning and purpose beneath the surface of things

3. **What is the meaning of "spiritual formation"?**

What does this term suggest to you? Write down what comes to mind:

Ponder this definition:

Spiritual formation is the process of being shaped according to the image of Christ by the gracious working of the Holy Spirit, for the sake of the world.[3]

SCRIPTURAL FOUNDATIONS FOR SPIRITUAL FORMATION

In the New Testament the goal of the spiritual life is our reshaping in the likeness of Jesus Christ, for the sake of the world God loves. We call the process of Christ being formed in us "spiritual formation."

Beloved, we are God's children now; what we will be has not yet been revealed. What we do know is this: . . . we will be like him [Christ] (1 John 3:2).

"Be perfect [mature, complete], therefore, as your heavenly Father is perfect" (Matt. 5:48).

"You shall love the Lord your God with all your heart, and with all your soul, and with all your strength, and with all your mind; and your neighbor as yourself" (Luke 10:27).

I am again in the pain of childbirth until Christ is formed in you (Gal. 4:19).

All of us . . . are being transformed into the same image [image of Christ] from one degree of glory to another (2 Cor. 3:18).

It is he [Christ] whom we proclaim . . . so that we may present everyone mature in Christ. For this I toil and struggle with all the energy that he powerfully inspires within me (Col. 1:28-29).

SPIRITUAL FORMATION DEFINITION

Spiritual formation is the process of being shaped according to the image of Christ by the gracious working of the Holy Spirit, for the sake of the world.

This definition corresponds to the central ideas of several spiritual writers, ancient and modern.

1. *Spiritual formation is a process:*
   - Gradual, lifelong development, not a single momentous conversion
   - No do-it-yourself, quick-fix, three-step program

2. *of being shaped according to the image of Christ:*
   - Christ is the image of God made visible to us (Col. 1:15).
   - Our lives are formed, for better or worse, by the influence of culture or by the influence of Christ and his Spirit; we are all misshapen by images of worldly culture.

3. *by the gracious working of the Holy Spirit:*
   - We can open ourselves to Christ and to the gracious working of the Holy Spirit.
   - Spiritual disciplines are ways of opening ourselves to the wind of the Spirit.

4. *for the sake of the world:*
   - Our spiritual formation is not just for our own benefit but for the good of all whom God can touch through us. We are to be salt and light in a world full of blandness and darkness.
   - Transformed persons are the leaven by which God changes the world.

Readings for Reflection

Sometimes it helps to hear others tell of how or when they began to think of their lives in terms of a spiritual path. The following true story may serve as a springboard to help you think about your life as a sacred journey.

WILD WEST REDEMPTION

It was truly by the grace of God and the loving hands of many people that I was rescued from a precarious life and invited to become part of a family.

My mother died when I was four, and for two years I roamed about the small town of Custer, South Dakota. I received some guidance from my grandmother, but she was very old and not well. I searched through garbage cans for food and often slept on pool tables in saloons where I was taken by my drunken stepfather.

Then, I was placed in a series of foster homes. I remember staying with a farm family that received funds from the state for my care. They seated me at a table away from the family and gave me leftovers after the family finished eating. At the age of six, weighing only twenty-five pounds, I suffered from malnutrition.

An act of God had brought together Ruby Nichols and Floyd Eugene Tyler, my last foster family. They had both been raised on farms in rural South Dakota. . . . During World War II they both served in the armed forces. Floyd, a Marine, was held as a prisoner of war for thirty-six months in the Philippines, and Ruby was in the Army in London.

In 1951, after living for a year with Ruby and Floyd, I was given a choice. It was a warm day in July, and the three of us were at the home of a judge who sat in a wheelchair. He looked at me and said, "Phyllis Fisher, would you like these two people to be your parents?" "Yes, yes, yes," I gleefully exclaimed, as I danced around the judge's chair. "Then your new name is Phyllis Tyler," he said with judicial authority.

I was given a new name, a new life, and a new hope on that day. I was brought from death to life, from no home to a home, from no family to a family. Even though I was quite young, from that moment I understood the grace of God. Complete joy encircled my malnourished body.

Several months later the Tyler family brought me to be baptized. As the water trickled down my forehead, I knew I was God's child. My adoption and baptism were signs of God's grace, of acceptance and delight in my being alive. Yes, God was pleased that I had been born. I was chosen to receive life, and now all I needed to do was to receive that gift and live fully each of the days that awaited me. And from that day forth, I have lived with a sense of gratitude for each day.[4]

Phyllis Tyler serves as pastor of Sage Granada Park United Methodist Church in Alhambra, California.

Taste and See

THE PRACTICE OF JOURNALING

Something in the physical act of writing releases creativity and self-understanding .... journaling unlocks the imagination.[5]

—Anne Broyles, *Journaling: A Spiritual Journey*

To "journal" means to record your thoughts, feelings, questions, and insights over time. There is a difference between keeping a diary and keeping a journal. And a typical journal differs from a spiritual journal. For example:

- A *diary* records events, facts, and occasions with little, if any, commentary: *Went to dinner and movie with Chelsea. Saw* Dead Man Walking.

- A *journal* records subjective responses to events in thoughts, feelings, and hopes:
  Dinner was great! Chelsea enjoyed it but seemed kind of preoccupied and restless. Wish we'd had more time to talk. The movie just blew us away. Really emotionally draining. Neither of us could say much afterward.

- A *spiritual journal* focuses on how thoughts and feelings relate to our faith experience. It moves to honest reflection on self and God, often flowing into spontaneous prayer.
  Can't fathom how Sister Prejean could relate to that man the way she did. I'd be more like the parents of the victim. Guess I have trouble seeing the humanity of a murderer. Does that make me an unforgiving person? I suspect Jesus would be more generous, willing to offer a chance at redemption. O God, help me see more with your eyes!

In a spiritual journal we note where we start out and track the growth in our life's journey toward God. We can journal:
- *in response to life experience*—becoming more aware of God's presence and guidance amidst daily circumstances.
- *through reflections on nature or the Bible*—pondering their messages.

- *in response to dreams*—listening for unconscious truths expressed in symbolic form by dreams.
- *by writing conversations we imagine having with God, others, or various parts of ourselves*—gaining insight into ourselves and God.

PRACTICAL MATTERS

Start small—just a few words or sentences are OK. Don't get bogged down in words.

Don't sweat the grammar—A journal is for *you*; you share from it only what you choose. Punctuation, spelling, grammar, even legibility are not important as long as you can read your own writing!

Find your own style—You need not be a writer; just be yourself. There's no right way to journal and no one will grade your work. Be creative if you like: doodle, scribble, write a poem or a joke. Let the Spirit move you, and don't be afraid to have some fun!

O taste and see that the Lord is good.
—Psalm 34:8

SIX SPIRITUAL PRACTICES FOR THE JOURNEY

These are the disciplines you will be introduced to over the course of these six weeks:

1. JOURNALING—tracking your faith experiences and responses in writing

2. SHARING SPIRITUAL JOURNEYS—learning to share facets of your faith journey with others for insight, support, and encouragement

3. *LECTIO DIVINA*—the classic practice of spiritual reading or "praying the scriptures"

4. BREATH PRAYER—a simple way to pray through the day with a short phrase

5. HOLY LISTENING—the practice of deep and attentive listening to one another

6. DAILY EXAMEN—looking back over a twenty-four-hour period with an eye to God's presence and your response in the day

Spiritual Exercises for the Week

By writing your reflections on the following questions this week, you can expand your experience with journaling (first key spiritual practice) and prepare to share something of your spiritual journey (second key spiritual practice) in next week's class. Use the journal pages at the back of this Participant's Book, a notebook, your own personal journal, or *Journal: A Companion for Your Quiet Time* (see Annotated Resource List, page 73). Focus on one question each day, and do as many exercises as you can this week.

1. What attracted you to this class? What are you looking for? What do you hope for? (Ask God to help you discover your inner aspirations.)

2. Ask yourself, *Where am I on my faith journey?* Look back at the time line you developed during the meeting. Add other significant turning points along the path of your life—points of change, insight, or questioning. What word, phrase, or symbol might describe your current location?

3. Use a time-line diagram to chart some of this week's events or experiences. What events fall "above the line"? What do you notice "below the line"?

4. What spiritual practices or "faith habits" have you tried at times? When have you prayed, read the Bible, shared questions or stories of faith with others, kept a diary, or in some way reflected regularly on your life? Which of these practices has been helpful to you or continues to be helpful?

5. When in your life (circumstances, settings, relationships) have you felt closest to God or had a deeper sense of faith?

6. Who in your life has most clearly demonstrated God's love to you? Who has most influenced your faith, and in what way?

Quotes for Further Reflection

Our "journey into Christ" is that lifelong process which our tradition has called sanctification—growth in holiness. But holiness is not some ephemeral, antiseptic state separated from our family, work, or life as a public citizen. It is absolutely practical and concrete. Holy people (saints) get into the dirt and sweat of real life, where light and darkness contend with real consequences. This is where God is at work.

—Marjorie Thompson, *Soul Feast*

In Christian spirituality, a discipline is a rule of life or a set pattern of living intended to facilitate spiritual growth and Christian community. . . . Among these patterns of living are some called the classical spiritual disciplines because they have biblical roots and because through the various ages and renewal movements of the church, Christians have tested them and found them central to experiential Christianity and growth toward spiritual maturity.

—*The Upper Room Dictionary of Christian Spiritual Formation*

Journal writing is a sharing between our true selves and the God of Truth. In journaling, we come to know ourselves as we really are and feel the acceptance of the One who loves us no matter what.

—Anne Broyles, *Journaling: A Spiritual Journey*

Week 2
Sharing the Adventure

For those blessed souls who are able to let go, to float free, a new and mysterious world is revealed. It is a world more mysterious, more exotic and, initially, more threatening than the new world Columbus and Magellan stumbled upon.[1]
—THOMAS H. GREEN, *When the Well Runs Dry*

Setting the Stage

1. **Review: Life is a sacred journey, the purpose of which is our spiritual formation.**

   "Spiritual formation is the process of being shaped according to the image of Christ by the gracious working of the Holy Spirit, for the sake of the world."

2. **Our sacred journeys are a lifelong adventure.**

   The difference between wandering and adventuring

Personal reflection questions:

- When have I undergone a positive change in my relationship with God or felt a new sense of adventure in my faith life?

- What spiritual practices or gifts have helped me in this shift?

3. God calls each of us to a closer relationship.

This relationship matures us, yet we are often afraid to respond to the call.

Negative and positive images of God

When has my image of God changed or matured?

4. **Three pictures of how we relate to God**

   • Pictograms:

God is "above us," "out there"; our job is to reach up, connect

God is within us, in our heart/soul

We live within God's being, can't exist apart from God

   • Implications of each pictogram for spiritual formation

5. **The role of spiritual disciplines**

   My understanding of the meaning of "spiritual disciplines"

   Theological perspectives on spiritual discipline

   Philippians 2:12-13—our cooperation with the Spirit already at work

6. **Three metaphors of spiritual discipline**

   wind and sail

   trellis

   creating space

Readings for Reflection

LISTENING FOR THE VOICE

To become a spiritual adventurer means learning to listen for the voice of God. This listening involves a certain level of risk and vulnerability that does not come easily. Here is the story of one woman who had many fears about really listening to God.

> I remember a woman I met on a late-night flight to Indianapolis. She was a brilliant, successful Ph.D. who had consulted with corporations and had been a presidential speech writer. She possessed unique and powerful gifts. She had accomplished more in her three and a half decades than many persons do in a lifetime. In our conversation she expressed her dread of self-confrontation. She described her fear of hearing a voice say, "All right, you have been given so much; now it is time for you to pay up."
>
> I wondered why she kept running away and asked, "Why don't you listen to the Voice?"
>
> Over the course of our hour-long conversation, she gave me three reasons: "I fear I would become a fanatic. . . . I don't want to be like one of them. I also have a fear I would shatter into a thousand pieces if I listened to and obeyed the voice of God. . . . But, to tell the truth, I am afraid to listen for God because I want to control my life. I have plans for my life, and I don't want God or anyone interfering with them."[2]

Questions for reflection

What are my fears about listening for God's voice?

What would it mean for me to risk truly listening to divine guidance?

A MODERN-DAY ADVENTURER

Ben Campbell Johnson, who wrote "Listening for the Voice," discovered in his own experience God's invitation into relationship. This discovery came about for him through the spiritual discipline of prayer.

One day a friend began to tell Ben about changes in his life that had come about through prayer. Ben wasn't so sure about the idea of a close relationship with God, but he was impressed by what his friend told him: Since meeting weekly to speak and listen to God with some other friends, virtually every person in the group had experienced remarkable answers to prayer. A couple on the verge of divorce was experiencing a deep healing in their relationship. Another person had undergone a physical healing. Ben's friend spoke with warmth, humor, and quiet assurance, sparking Ben's hunger to know more.

A few weeks later, Ben's friend put a small book on prayer into his hands. It was written by W. E. Sangster, an eminent preacher and popular devotional writer in England during World War II. The book described a simple pattern of morning and evening prayer, fifteen minutes in the morning and ten minutes in the evening. Still skeptical, Ben decided as an experiment to give the pattern a week's try just to see if it made any difference in his life. He tried it out faithfully, and by the end of one week began to feel differently about what he was doing. He didn't feel the same kind of resistance or skepticism and found that he wanted to continue. By the end of two weeks, he began to feel something new arising in him. He had a sense of God's real presence with him, not only during times of prayer but throughout the day; he began to feel more centered instead of scattered in his daily activities; and "coincidences" began to occur more frequently.[3]

Taste and See

GUIDELINES FOR SHARING
SPIRITUAL JOURNEYS

When sharing aspects of our faith life or spiritual journey with others, the following reminders grant freedom of expression, as well as freedom to listen. Those who listen may accept, refuse, agree, or disagree and still receive care and loving respect.

- Speak only for yourself. Don't assume that others share your experiences, interpretations, values, or choices.

- Offer your story as a gift, expecting no return. Do not be surprised if some respond positively and others do not.

- Accept that people are at different points on their journeys and that God works with each person differently.

- Let your story speak its own language to the hearts of others. Refrain from trying to teach theology or to draw general lessons for others from your words.

- Pray for the grace of honesty in your sharing. We learn to be authentic human beings as we risk taking off our social masks with other caring believers.

- Be discreet and appropriate in self-disclosure. Revealing more than others need to know can get boring. This is not therapy time.

Spiritual Exercises for the Week

In class this week you got a taste of sharing your faith journey by telling a little about your spiritual life. This week expand the circle of persons with whom you share your faith stories and invite others to tell you their stories.

1. Try sharing some aspect of your faith journey with a person outside your class (a church member, family member, friend, coworker). You might introduce the subject with a tie-in you both know: "Last night I saw a movie (video, TV show) that made me think about God (or, my spiritual life) in a new way. I wonder what you think of this . . . ?" Or gain practice in speaking about your faith by asking, "Would you be willing to listen to me share some of my journey?"

2. Ask a person of faith to share a meaningful event from his or her own spiritual journey: perhaps a time of sensing God's presence, an experience in which he or she questioned God, or some turning point. You might begin the conversation with a question to prime the pump, such as: "How has your faith grown during your life?" or "What experiences have most deepened your belief?"

3. Note in your journal pages any insights you gain from one or both of these times of sharing. Was a given exercise difficult, rewarding, or both? Why? If you both shared and listened, which was easier for you to do? How did you sense God's presence during these times of sharing with others?

4. Ponder your primary image of God. Spend some time meditating with one of the scripture texts below that assure us of God's personal love. Allow yourself to sink into the heart of God's love for you, and simply rest there without struggling to deserve or resist it. Let God's love come fully inside. After some time, write in your journal pages what comes to mind.

Hosea 11:1-4	John 3:16	Romans 8:31-39
Luke 15:4-7	Luke 15:8-10	Luke 15:11-32

Quotes for Further Reflection

For those blessed souls who are able to let go, to float free, a new and mysterious world is revealed. It is a world more mysterious, more exotic and, initially, more threatening than the new world Columbus and Magellan stumbled upon. Those who "stay home" will only know of it by hearsay, and will scarcely believe what they hear. The few whom grace and their own generosity launch on the uncharted sea—they alone will ever really know whether the explorers' tales are true.

—Thomas H. Green, *When the Well Runs Dry*

Discipline in the Christian life is not a luxury. Without it we become confused, lose our way, compromise our principles, and discover that we are not the people we had intended to be. . . . These tools, or aids, are ways by which we open ourselves to God's free grace. . . . They give our Christian pilgrimage a definite shape.

—Howard Rice, *Reformed Spirituality*

What I am writing you is my story—my spiritual journey from childhood beliefs through times of much questioning and discarding, to the rediscovery of Jesus and a maturing faith. I am trying to be as honest as I know how, but, of course, my journey will not be yours. Each must discover God, or more accurately, each must place himself or herself before the Creator of the universe and discover that he or she is loved—dearly loved—and called by name. Ours is a very personal as well as universal God whose name is Love.

—Mary Virginia Parrish, *No Stopping Place*

Week 3

Bread for the Journey

Scripture is like a river, broad and deep, shallow enough here for the lamb to go wading,
but deep enough there for the elephant to swim.[1]
—GREGORY THE GREAT (540–604), *Moralia in Iob, Book I*

Setting the Stage

1. **Review: Last week we explored the role of spiritual disciplines in our lifelong adventure of being on the spiritual journey.** We shared our spiritual journeys with one another as a way to pay attention to God's presence and guidance in our lives. Today we will talk about a way to read the Bible that helps us listen to God's word for us.

2. **Gregory the Great's image of scripture—the shallows and the depths**

    Gregory the Great (540–604 CE) spoke of the scriptures metaphorically as a river that was both shallow enough for a lamb to wade in and deep enough for an elephant to swim in. (*You may want to sketch the diagram your leader draws in the space provided below.*)

Swimming in the shallows / informational approach to scripture

Launching into the depths / formational approach to scripture

3. Meditating on God's word: *lectio divina*

Reading

Reflecting

Responding

Resting

Readings for Reflection

This week we are reflecting on the place of scripture in our faith journey. You have an opportunity to think more about your relationship to the book we call God's Word and to test again the ways of meditating with scripture that you briefly experienced in class.

Some of us have a less positive sense of the Bible than others. My ninety-year-old mother-in-law grew up in a strict Calvinist household. She remembers, at age four or five, going to her grandparents' house every Sunday after church. There, she and her older sister were made to sit on stools at the feet of their grandmother. Garbed in a stiff, high-collared black dress, their grandmother read the Bible to these little girls for a whole hour! My mother-in-law developed a strong emotional block against the Bible from a tender age. She still has trouble hearing anything in it other than archaic words.

Thankfully, many of us have grown up with more positive impressions of the Bible. Even so, some Christians assume the Bible as background; it is familiar territory, yet has never really come alive as a vital source of personal connection with God. *Exploring the Way* can help us gain a new appreciation for the place of scripture in our lives, not just as interesting information but as a medium of communication in a real, ongoing relationship with God.

Below, one person describes this way of relating to God's Word:

A NOTE ON THE DOOR

I think of praying the scriptures in very personal terms. I like to think of it as if I had come home from a day at work to find a note on the front door from Marcie, my wife. As I unlock the front door, I see the note and read it. "Steve, don't go anywhere until I get home. —Marcie."

I open the door, sit down in a chair, and read it again. I read it with great attention because it is from my wife, someone very important to me. But I begin to wonder what the note means. Does she mean, "Steve, don't go anywhere because I want to spend some special time with you"? Or does she mean, "Steve, don't go anywhere because you are in trouble"? I know the note means something specific, but I cannot know what it means without asking her.

As I am sitting there thinking, suddenly the door opens and in walks Marcie. I no longer ask myself, "What does she mean?" Now I turn to her and ask, "What do you mean? What are you wanting to say to me?" She says, "We need to talk. We need to spend some time talking about our relationship."

I start making excuses, but she continues to tell me that we need to talk about our relationship. Eventually, we do talk, and after a time we have said everything we need to say. Then we are able to rest, simply be quiet in each other's presence. Finally, based on our discussion we take some action, hopefully action that will improve our relationship.

Praying the scriptures is like this story. When I pray the scriptures, first I read and reread the words carefully, since the Bible is important to me. Secondly, I reflect on its possible meanings for my life. I believe the words of scripture are like a letter from God— they have particular meaning for my life, just as I trust a note from Marcie has a special meaning for me. Then I enter into dialogue with the passage and ask God what the grace or truth are that I need to receive.

After I have finished reflecting on what a passage says to me, I have an opportunity to rest in the word, acknowledging the sovereignty of God. Finally, praying the scriptures moves me to action. It reminds me of the importance of my relationship with God and encourages me to build that relationship and live in the world as a child of God.[2]

One of the points this story makes is that meditating on the Bible, or "praying the scriptures," is like listening to a personal message from someone very dear to us. The great twentieth-century theologian Dietrich Bonhoeffer makes this same point in his book *Meditating on the Word*:

When a dear friend speaks a word to us, do we subject it to analysis? No, we simply accept it, and then it resonates inside us for days. The word of someone we love opens itself up to us the more we "ponder it in our hearts," as Mary did. In the same way, we should carry the Word of the Bible around with us. We will only be happy in our reading of the Bible when we dare to approach it as the means by which God really speaks to us, the God who loves us and will not leave us with our questions unanswered.[3]

Of course, when we try to meditate on God's word—in fact, when we set aside time for any kind of prayer—we often find ourselves distracted with many seemingly unrelated thoughts. Our minds are like buzzing mosquitoes or monkeys jumping around in banana trees! How do we deal with the obstacles our own minds throw out that can prevent us from quality time with God? Here is some experienced advice:

One of the more specific obstacles encountered in spiritual reading is lack of attention. You seek to still yourself, to be open to the Word. You read the text, you reread it, you reread it, and suddenly you discover you are thinking about last night's television show or the meeting coming up tomorrow or the children who need braces on their teeth. Life intrudes. You realize you are sitting there, and your eyes are going through the motions of running over the words on the page, but your being is somewhere else.

Don't fight this experience; your resistance will just make your inattention stronger. Instead, calmly, steadily, gently but persistently return to the text. Start again to still and open yourself before the text and focus your attention on the passage before you. If you again find yourself going off in another direction, just firmly return to the text and begin reading again. As often as distractions intrude or your attention wanders, return to the text, to opening yourself to God, and to being still before the Word. If you are persistent, gradually you will develop the ability to still yourself before the Word and to "be there" with God.[4]

JIM'S STORY

In his book *Prayer: Finding the Heart's True Home*, Richard J. Foster tells the story of a bright young student named Jim. While in graduate school Jim decided to go on a private retreat to help revitalize his spiritual life. The monk assigned to be his spiritual director gave him a simple assignment: to meditate on Luke's story of the Annunciation.

The first day, aiming to better understand the text, Jim analyzed the passage and came up with several insights. His spiritual director was not impressed. The monk told him to continue with the same passage, reading with his heart not just his head. Jim tried all the next day with no success. He told his director that he couldn't do what he was being asked to do. The monk replied, "You're trying too hard. . . . Don't manipulate God; just receive. . . . It's like sleep. You can't make yourself sleep, but you can create the conditions that allow sleep to happen."

After further effort, Jim despaired and gave up. He felt no connection at all with God and began weeping. After a time, he looked once more at the all-too-familiar story in his Bible, but now somehow it seemed different. Mary's words started to become his own: "Let it be to me. . . . " Then an inner dialogue with God began about his life and Mary's, his fears and hers. Many feelings surfaced. The angel's words to Mary seemed also to be spoken to him: "You have found favor with God." His heart was opened wide to the grace and love of his Lord.

In losing "control" he rediscovered the God he felt he had lost and began the recovery of his own lost self.[5]

Taste and See

A PROCESS FOR PERSONAL *LECTIO DIVINA*

Preparation: Select a text for the session. Many use the lectionary readings or some thematic scheme. Take a moment to quiet the heart and mind in preparation to encounter God by using a deep breathing relaxation technique or just two or three minutes of silence.

LECTIO—Hearing the Sacred Word

The emphasis during this portion is on "hearing" God address you personally through the sacred text. The method suggests three slow readings.

First Reading: Read the entire passage slowly, allowing each word to speak to you. Pause often between words or verses. Sit silently for a minute or two.

Second Reading: Reread the passage, again slowly with pauses to allow a word or phrase or image in the text to call you to attention. This time make a mental note of the word, phrase, or image in the text that caught your attention. Again sit in silence.

Third Reading: Reread the passage up to the point you are touched by a word or verse. You have found the word or verse in the scripture that God desires to speak to you in a personal way. At this point the process will flow into the next step of meditation.

MEDITATIO—Pondering the Personal Word

The emphasis in this step is on pondering the word or verse that touched you in the *lectio*. Pondering is like memorizing by repeating the word or verse gently to yourself. Allow the word to sink into your consciousness through a playful interaction with your thoughts, hopes, memories, imagination, desires, and fears. In this movement God can speak the individual personal word to your specific condition. The fullness of this encounter flows naturally into the next step of vocal prayer.

ORATIO—Intimate Dialogue with God

Often the spontaneous vocal prayer that flows from the heart of meditation is an expression of love, praise, or thanksgiving. However, it is usually experienced as an intimate dialogue with God, a gentle movement between heartfelt expressions and responsiveness to the movements of the Spirit nurtured by deeper meditation.

CONTEMPLATIO—Heavenly Rest

Eventually a gradual simplification comes from the space created by vocal prayer, and your words begin to lack true expressive qualities. The heart and mind become still and silent. You simply rest and enjoy the experience of being in God's presence. You stop "doing" and learn to enjoy "being."[6]

Spiritual Exercises for the Week

In class this week you had a taste of *lectio divina*, a classic approach to meditating with scripture, or "praying the Bible." Now you have a chance to explore this method on your own, taking as much time as you want or can afford. In addition, the first exercise below guides you in using the imagination in meditating on scripture.

First, be sure to find a quiet space apart. Take steps to minimize distractions and interruptions: turn off the TV, radio, and phone ringer (or use the phone answering machine); tell your family or roommate that you are not available for the next twenty to thirty minutes. Give yourself permission to enter the gift of solitude and silence for a time. Prepare to listen inwardly to God's Word.

1. Read Mark 14:3-9, the story of the woman who anoints Jesus. Imagine yourself there in the room with Jesus, those gathered, and the woman. What do you see, hear, smell, taste, touch, and feel inwardly? You might try identifying with various people in the scene to see if you sense things differently from their standpoint. Note your responses in your journal pages.

2. Try out the personal *lectio divina* process (page 36) with either Psalm 23 or Psalm 139:1-18 (Focus on no more than six verses from Psalm 139). Be sure to take time for the fourth stage: resting in God and allowing yourself simply to be. Write a few words in your journal pages about how you experience this way of entering the Bible. Include fresh insights or questions that may have come to you in your meditation.

   Remember the four *R*s:

   • Reading

   • Reflecting

   • Responding

   • Resting

3. Try out *lectio* again, this time with Romans 8:26-27 or 8:37-39. Again, do not neglect the fourth stage of *contemplatio*. Record your thoughts in your journal pages.

Quotes for Further Reflection

Read the Bible as though it were something entirely unfamiliar, as though it had not been set before you ready made. . . . Face the book with a new attitude as something new. . . . Let whatever may happen occur between yourself and it. You do not know which of its sayings and images will overwhelm you and mold you. . . . But hold yourself open. . . . Read aloud the words written in the book in front of you, hear the word you utter, and let it reach you.

—Martin Buber, Lecture 1929

There are some who may have to overcome an experience of having the Bible used as a weapon to make them conform.

—Elizabeth Canham, *Heart Whispers*

The simplest and most basic way to meditate upon the text of Scripture is through the imagination. . . . We are desiring to see, to hear, to touch the biblical narrative. In this simple way we begin to enter the story and make it our own. We move from detached observation to active participation.

—Richard Foster, *Prayer: Finding the Heart's True Home*

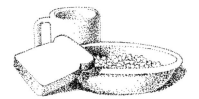

Week 4
Drink for the Journey

Perhaps our real task in prayer is to attune ourselves to the conversation already going on deep in our hearts. Then we may align our conscious intentions with the desire of God being expressed at our core.[1]
—MARJORIE THOMPSON, *Soul Feast*

Setting the Stage

1. **Review: Last week we explored meditation on scripture as a spiritual practice that takes us beyond the usual limits of Bible study.** Meditating is a way of pondering the Word. As we listen for God's voice in scripture, we become more familiar with the sound of God's voice in our lives and hearts.

2. **Another great gift for our spiritual journey, closely related to meditation, is prayer.**

3. **Our typical experience with prayer**

   Prayer is an aspect of our faith life we often take for granted.

Our typical way of viewing prayer leaves us with many unanswered questions.

4. The larger picture of prayer

Prayer is far more than asking for what we want.

Prayer is an openness to God's gracious presence in our world, at work in our lives.

Readings for Reflection

SOME THOUGHTS ON PRAYER

One of the points made in class this week is that prayer is not primarily an obligation or duty but a living relationship. If we think of prayer as mere discipline, we miss the vivid sense of an ongoing journey of companionship with our Best Friend, of guidance from our Wisest Counselor, of communion with our Loving Creator.

Flora Slosson Wuellner speaks to this understanding, inviting us to move beyond rigid or constraining ways we may have been taught to view and practice prayer:

THE DOOR OF PRAYER

God, the eternal healer, the eternal lover, offers to touch our tiredness, our stress, and our pain. The most direct response to this love, the widest door we can open, is through the relationship we call prayer. For it is a relationship and not primarily a discipline.

Most of our problems with prayer arise from our tendency to turn spiritual growing into a set of laws or a gymnastic exercise. I have seen great inner struggle, fatigue, and guilt result when we treat prayer like a discipline. . . .

It is best to have some form of deliberate opening to God each day, but we need not be troubled if the form and expression change. That is as it should be. God's love is a growing personal relatedness in which we are loved and challenged to love without limit. *This transforming friendship always nurtures before it challenges as well as during the challenge.*[2]

How are we to cultivate this transforming friendship? It is one thing to develop a relationship with a friend, spouse, child, or coworker. In human relationships we can see, hear, and touch one another. We learn how to interpret others' facial expressions and physical gestures, inflections of voice and mood tones. What do we have to build on in developing a relationship with God—invisible, mysterious, and often inscrutable? How do we learn communication skills with One who is personal yet not merely human like us?

The place to begin is with silence, an external condition of quiet that calms the turbulence of our mind and heart. In the stillness, over time, we begin to learn a new language of the spirit—a language our souls already know but that we have forgotten. One writer describes her experience with silence this way:

THE GIFT OF SILENCE

The gift of silence puts us in touch with an inner place where we are truly alive. While cultural messages teach us that fulfillment comes by accumulating more—and then still more—silence teaches us the paradox that to be emptied is to be filled, to let go is to possess. When we sit alone in the quiet, letting go of our struggles, concerns, compulsions, and insistence upon having things go "our way," we are filled with the One for whom we deeply hunger. Silence wakes us up to the One who is Life and Love. This is prayer.[3]

Silence. *Well and good*, we may think. *But my life is too busy to take time like this daily. A few moments here and there, yes, but twenty minutes or an hour in silence? I can see how it might be a good thing, but I've got to be realistic! After all, I'm no monk.*

The challenge of finding time for listening prayer in our increasingly hectic lives is tremendous. It may help to remember that we have choices about how we use the time given to us and that we set our priorities based on what we value most. If we really value our relationship with God (which happens to be the most important relationship in the world, whether or not we are aware of it), we will make time to be with God just as we make time to be with the people who are most important to us.

But the question of time has another aspect to it. Often time is given to us in ways we would not choose: we get stuck in a slow line behind ten people at the checkout counter; our flight is delayed by an hour; we get sick enough to require bed rest for several days. Then the question is, What do we do with such time? One answer can be found in the story that follows:

LOCKED OUT

Click. The door closed behind me. I'm locked out, I realized in dismay. I turned the knob, but it didn't budge. In my hurry, I'd left my keys inside. It would be hours before my husband came home from work.

Frustration set in as I contemplated the long stretch of time ahead of me. If there's anything I detest, it's sitting around waiting for something to happen. But now I was forced to do just that.

On top of everything, it was a sweltering summer afternoon—much too hot to move around in. I found a shady place where I could figure a way out of my dilemma. It wasn't an emergency, so I didn't feel the need to impose upon my neighbors for help. The only other solution was to break a window, but that seemed a bit drastic. My car keys were also inside. No car, no travel. It was hopeless. I had no choice but to wait.

Settling down for the duration, I began observing the beauty of the landscape. Despite the constant heat, we'd had enough rain to keep everything a luscious green. I had much to be thankful for—a wonderful husband, a beautiful home in the country, a fine church, and good friends.

This morning, in a rush to get to church to help with a children's project, I'd neglected to pray and have my usual devotions. Could getting locked out of my house be God's way of getting my attention? God had it now, regardless.

As my thoughts began focusing on God, the fact that I couldn't do any of the things I thought so important gradually drifted into the background. The verse from Psalm 46:10 came to mind: "Be still, and know that I am God!" Different people began coming to mind. I prayed for their needs as they came up—the students in my Sunday school class, church friends, and one after another, family members.

My former pastor had once said, "We don't need an appointment to talk to God." That's true, but I wonder how many times I'd acted as if God needed one to speak with me. I'd been putting God on my mental appointment calendar. When my schedule became hectic, I would spend limited time with God, or like earlier today, no time at all.

I'd been taking God for granted, accepting blessings without showing my appreciation. I had locked God out of my day, just as I had locked myself out of my house. Now everything on my schedule had come to a halt, except communing with God.

A light breeze stirred in the trees overhead. I looked at my watch. Over an hour had gone by since my mad dash out of the house. I felt at peace with the Lord and myself.

Time alone with God had renewed my spiritual energy. I felt grateful God had used my rushing around to highlight my priorities and turned my waiting into waiting on God.[4]

Taste and See

DISCOVERING YOUR BREATH PRAYER

A breath prayer is a short prayer phrase that can be carried in memory through the day. It is called "breath prayer" because the Hebrew word for *breath* and *spirit* are the same word and because prayer is to be as natural as breathing. It expresses a deep desire of the heart before God over time.

Begin by closing your eyes and quieting yourself. Remember that you are resting in God's loving presence and that God cares deeply for you.

Imagine God calling you by name and asking, "(*Your name*), what do you most want?"

Answer God honestly with whatever word or phrase comes from deep within you.

Then choose your favorite or most natural name for God.

Combine your word or phrase of desire with your favorite name for God to form a brief prayer of six to eight syllables that flow smoothly. For example:

What I Want	My Name for God	Possible Prayer
Peace	God	Let me know your peace, O God.
Love	Jesus	Jesus, let me feel your love.
Rest	Shepherd	My Shepherd, let me rest in you.
Guidance	Eternal Light	Eternal Light, guide me in your way.

Repeat the prayer for a few minutes, allowing the words to settle into a peaceful rhythm.

Try praying it during quiet moments in your day. Carry the prayer into daily activities such as household chores, taking a walk, or waiting in traffic. Pay attention to how God uses your prayer to reshape your perceptions and calm your spirit.

Spiritual Exercises for the Week

Today's class introduced you to a form of prayer called "breath prayer." This week give yourself some sustained time with your breath prayer as well as the opportunity to practice being quiet in God's presence. For the latter, find a quiet personal space where you will not be interrupted for a period of time. Minimize the possibility of external distractions, and let yourself receive the gift of this prayer.

1. Get into a position that feels relaxed but will help you stay aware and alert. Sitting with your spine straight, feet flat on the floor, eyes closed, and hands open works well for most people. Take several slow breaths and let your muscles relax. Still the activity of your mind by focusing on your favorite name for God or by focusing attention on your breathing, remembering that the Hebrew word for "breath" and "spirit" are one. As you become quiet and still inside, allow yourself to be held gently in God's love and light. Just be still and receive whatever God wants to give you.

2. Practice your breath prayer for ten to fifiteen minutes. Consider practicing while sitting, walking, washing dishes, folding laundry, watering plants, or working out (any activity that occupies only the surface of your mind and that won't involve interacting with others). Note in your journal pages what it is like to pray this way. What difficulties, questions, or insights come to you?

3. Share your breath prayer with someone you love, and ask that person to pray your prayer with and for you. Or invite someone to discover his or her own breath prayer with your help, and offer to pray it with and for that person. Note in your journal pages any changes in your perceptions of daily life over the next several days.

Quotes for Further Reflection

The art of praying, as we grow, is really the art of learning to waste time gracefully—to be simply the clay in the hands of the potter. This may sound easy—too easy to be true—but it is really the most difficult thing we ever learn to do.

—Thomas Green, *When the Well Runs Dry*

Within us all there is a yearning that nothing—no thing, no created object, no person, no pleasure—can satisfy. We are athirst for the living God.

—David Rensberger, *Weavings*

Perhaps our real task in prayer is to attune ourselves to the conversation already going on deep in our hearts. Then we may align our conscious intentions with the desire of God being expressed at our core.

—Marjorie Thompson, *Soul Feast*

Week 5

Companions on the Way

The spiritual life is not only a life of relationship with God, but it's also facilitated, encouraged, and shaped by the people we journey with. In other words it's not a privatized journey. It happens in community.[1]
—WENDY WRIGHT, *Alive Now*

Setting the Stage

1. **Review: Last week we explored prayer as a means of grace that opens our minds and hearts to the living God.** We discovered and practiced our breath prayer, a way to pray "unceasingly" through the day. This week we will see how being attentive to one another can help us be attentive to God's presence.

2. **Community offers us an essential gift for the Christian spiritual journey.**
   - God offers us an incredibly valuable gift in one another.

   - We are not meant to travel the path of life alone.

3. **Why is a community of believers important to spiritual growth?**
   - Community teaches us by experience how interdependent we are for spiritual health and vitality.

- The development of close friendships helps us mature in faith.

- Authentic community is a safe place to share questions, struggles, hopes, joys.

- We can help hold one another accountable to our spiritual commitments.

- We learn to respect others and celebrate common ground.

- Spiritual community provides a place to seek perspective on and guidance for deep or disturbing spiritual experiences.

- God often speaks to us through others.

Taste and See

PRINCIPLES OF HOLY LISTENING

Listening deeply to another person places us on sacred ground. The person we pay attention to is a child of God, made in the divine image. Moreover, God is present with us when we listen deeply to one of God's precious sons or daughters. So we can also listen for God as we listen to the other person. We can pay attention to how God is present for and through the other, and how God is present to us personally in the time of listening.

In any conversation with another person, but especially around matters of faith, you can practice these basic preparations and principles of listening:

- Take a few slow breaths, remembering who you and the other person are in God's sight: beloved children of God. Allow yourself to be aware of the divine presence and invite the Spirit to help you listen well.

- Set aside your own agenda. Give your whole attention to the other person. If you have ideas, feelings, or advice you wish to communicate, hold them for later. Ask clarifying questions only if you need to.

- Look into the other person's eyes with warmth and receptivity. Indicate by your physical posture that you are available to listen. Let your hands and feet be relaxed. You need not keep constant eye contact, but let it be with an open, loving look when your eyes meet.

- Listen with your heart as well as your head. Attend to the feelings and mood expressed in the other person's posture, gestures, and tone of voice. The words being spoken are only part of the whole message being communicated.

- Try to remain aware of God's presence with you both. Breathe little prayers of praise, gratitude, or supplication as you feel so moved in the course of listening to the other person.

- At the end of your time together, thank the other person for the opportunity to hear his or her story, viewpoints, or struggles. Indicate that you are enriched for getting to know him or her more fully.

- Jot down some notes in your journal on what you learn by listening in this way.

Readings for Reflection

This week we explore the gift of community in our Christian journey. Since we live in a culture that tends to idolize individual character and achievement, truly learning to value community can be a challenge for us. Here is the voice of one author, describing community's centrality to Christian growth and discipleship.

LESSONS OF COMMUNITY

As you [consider] your life, you can no doubt think of many things that you learned by watching, learning, and then imitating. This is how we learn to ride a bike, drive a car, and lift weights. It is also how we learn to "act cool" in high school, move up the social ladder in adulthood, and age gracefully in older years. In short, we learn about life in community.

The Christian life is exactly the same. There is no example in the Bible of a lone disciple. Even Paul, after his dramatic conversion and long stay in the desert, went to Jerusalem and associated himself with the apostles and later with the church at Antioch (Acts 9:26-30; 11:25-26). When he planted churches he always traveled in the company of others. He had a team relationship at different times with Barnabas, Silas, and Timothy. The relational, community-based model of disciplemaking had been demonstrated by Jesus and the disciples, and it provided the necessary support for Paul and the early church in the turbulent period after Pentecost.

Since we learn best in relationship, we most effectively learn to be disciples that way. But disciples produced through loving community in churches are too rare. The self-sufficient individualism of Western culture has seeped into the church and led to situations in which individuals are trying, often without notable success, to mature alone as disciples. Many resources—Christian books, videos, conferences, tape series—are available for these lone disciples to increase their knowledge about Jesus, but an accumulation of facts and ideas is only the beginning of Bible-based disciplemaking.

It takes a community of fellow disciples who can help each other learn to live a life transformed by the Holy Spirit. . . . Without a community in which we can learn, practice, fail and eventually move out from as agents of change, we are left without a secure foundation. Without a foundation of community, the church will ultimately fail.[2]

Some of us may ask, how does the church become such a loving community, one that fosters our freedom to "learn, practice, fail," try again, and gradually become the kind of person who truly follows Jesus? Some of our churches are judging communities, places where we would never reveal our deep questions, hurts, or weaknesses for fear of being labeled or rejected.

One of the chief structures within church life that allows us to mature as persons of faith is the small group. Small groups can take many forms and meet for various purposes, but they share common features: in them, Christians can begin to share who they are, their beliefs and struggles. They begin to establish trust with other members and to talk about their needs, dreams, and witness to faith.

Many people with the courage to commit to a small group have found that God becomes more real to them in the process. It may help to listen to the voices of a few such persons, speaking from their own experience.

Far away, in another part of the world, a woman named Janet joined a small group of South Africans—black and white—who have now met together for several years to read and study the Bible, pray, share their stories, and support one another. Here is her witness to the value of othis discipline:

> Twenty-six years ago I gave my life to Jesus Christ; but only in the past three and a half years as I walked with Jesus in the company of fellow Christians in a covenant group have I discovered the true meaning of "being a Christian." The covenantal journey calls for accountability to God and to each person in the group. This has been both life-changing and life-giving for me. I have been able to respond as a disciple of Christ to others, both within and outside of the group.[3]

Another woman named Kathleen found that the search for healthy small groups was well worth the effort:

> While the work of bringing our different personalities together into healthy, humane group-ings requires a leap of faith that is difficult in our culture, it is worth all the work to harvest the fruits of the spirit we may cultivate. . . . The small group experience offers rich sacred ground.[4]

Spiritual Exercises for the Week

In class you were given an exercise in Holy Listening to try with a partner. This week, you will probably have many opportunities to practice listening to someone: a spouse, child, friend, colleague, or stranger. Since all true communication is grounded in careful, attentive listening, this is an important spiritual practice to learn well. Our ability to listen deeply affects all our relationships for the better. So do yourself a favor. Experiment with one or more of the following exercises this week.

1. Review the "Principles of Holy Listening," pages 51–52. Ponder and absorb the basic ideas and the overall process. Then choose someone you live with daily (or a close friend, if you live alone) to practice listening to. You need not tell the person in advance what you are up to. Just be alert to a natural occasion for you to listen in this way. If need be, ask a nonthreatening, open-ended question to start the flow. (With older children and teens, it may be easier to sit or walk side by side with little direct eye contact.) Give at least five to ten minutes of uninterrupted listening to this family member (or friend). If it seems natural and appropriate during this time, you might ask another open-ended question directly related to what you are hearing.

    Be sure to note in your journal pages any reflections on how you experienced this listening time and what the response of the other person seemed to be. Ask yourself how aware you were of God in the process.

2. Review the "Principles of Holy Listening" pages again, absorbing the basic ideas and process. Then choose to listen to someone outside your circle of intimate relationships—perhaps a friend, coworker, or more general acquaintance.

    Again, note how you experience this process of listening and how the other person responds. Ponder your level of awareness of God's presence. Reflect on the difference between these two listening experiences.

3. Settle yourself peacefully someplace where you won't be interrupted. Spend ten minutes in quiet, listening for the voice of God prompting or gently stirring your spirit. What do you hear or sense?

    After your time of quiet listening, ask God to show you where/when/to whom you listen well and where/when/to whom you need to listen more fully. Bring to God your difficulties in listening: fears, feelings, or struggles. Listen for God's response. Make some journal notes on what you hear. You might want to write a prayer.

Quotes for Further Reflection

What happiness, what security, what joy to have someone to whom you dare to speak on terms of equality . . . one to whom you need have no fear to confess your failings; one to whom you can unblushingly make known what progress you have made in the spiritual life!

—Aelred of Rievaulx, twelfth century, *Spiritual Friendship*

Spiritual friendship . . . is typically more mutual and equal than other forms of guidance and has as its end shared encouragement in the love of God.

—Wendy Wright, *The Upper Room Dictionary of Spiritual Formation*

Each of us needs spiritual companionship and community to support—and sometimes to challenge—us. . . . We are, unfortunately, fallible beings capable of hearing what we want to hear, instead of God's true call. A spiritual community helps us stay on the right path.

—Debra Farrington, *Alive Now*

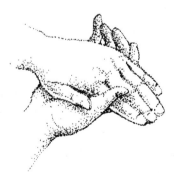

Week 6
Reaching Out in Love

Helping another reminds us that the goal of Christian growth is greater than our own warm feeling. It reminds us that God cares deeply about a whole world of people. . . . Our growth should be shared with others.[1]
—TIMOTHY JONES, *Finding a Spiritual Friend*

Setting the Stage

1. **Review: Our formation in Christ is "for the sake of the world," not merely for our own personal well-being.**

   Everything we have talked about and experienced over these weeks leads us to listen to God's call and to act on that call in relation to the world.

   - Journaling

   - Sharing our faith stories

   - Meditating on scripture (*lectio divina*)

   - Breath prayer

   - Holy listening

   Where is God calling us to reach out in love, to be the presence of Christ?

   - The gift of the world

   - Our God-given mission

   - Christian vocation

2. **Listening deeply prepares us to respond faithfully.**

   The biblical refrain "hear and obey" implies moving toward what is heard.

   As we listen to the voice of God's love, our response is shaped by love.

3. **Who are the "neighbors" Jesus invites us to reach out to?**

   "This love of our neighbour is the only door out of the dungeon of self."[2] (George Mac-Donald)

   List potential "neighbors"

   Recall stories of Jesus' reaching out in his ministry

   How might you reach out to such a neighbor?

4. Move from a sense of life's work as career to work as vocation (calling).

I have a God-given purpose, a personal mission in the world.

"God doesn't call the qualified, but qualifies the called."

Christian vocation involves hearing and responding to God's call in ordinary daily life—"practicing the presence of God."

5. Practicing the presence of God in daily life

Examples from class

Introduction to daily examen, or self-examination

Taste and See

DAILY EXAMEN

The examen, a form of self-examination, refers to a brief practice of reviewing the day's thoughts, feelings, and actions in relation to God's presence. This practice works best in the evening before you retire for the night but can be used at other times of day by reviewing the past twenty-four hours.

The version of examen described below is based on the teaching of Ignatius of Loyola and takes the form of direct prayer. Allow yourself to be guided by these prayers:

God, my Creator, I am totally dependent on you. Everything I am and have is your gift to me. Thank you for the gifts of this day. I praise you for your generous grace!

Holy Spirit, you work through time to reveal me to myself. Increase my awareness of how you are guiding and shaping my life, and make me sensitive to the obstacles I put in your way.

You have been present in my life today. Be near now as I reflect on these things:

- Your presence in the people and events of this day
- Your presence in the feelings I experienced today
- Your call to me
- My response to you

God, I ask your loving forgiveness and healing. What I most desire healing for today is

_____.

Filled with hope and faith in your love and power, I entrust myself to your care, and affirm that you desire to give me _____ (the gift you most need).[3]

Readings for Reflection

OUR CALL TO DISCIPLESHIP IN THE WORLD

This week we have begun to explore the gift of God's world in Christian spiritual growth. All around us we find a world full of profound needs and potential. That same world offers a vast array of resources to meet needs and fill potential. How will we offer ourselves and our gifts to meet the needs of our time? Are we willing to join others in community to pool resources and constructive ideas? The way we face the world as followers of Jesus Christ shapes our continued spiritual growth and shows the world what it means to belong to the body of Christ.

Two stories may help illustrate this dimension of the spiritual life. One story belongs to an individual, the other to a congregation. Both depict God's call to reach out to others with the love of Christ.

A CALL IN THE NIGHT

So often when God has called on me, it has been an inopportune time in my life. I usually feel inadequate and want to cry, "I can't do this, Lord." That was how I felt after I was awakened by the strident ring of the phone at three o'clock one morning. I fought panic as I hurried to answer. Nothing is more frightening to a mother whose children are away from home.

An unfamiliar voice with slurred speech hesitantly asked, "Could you . . . just talk to me?"

My first impulse was to hang up. But the note of sheer hopelessness in his voice told me this was not a prank call.

"Are you a student in one of my adult education classes?" I asked.

He was not. The young man was a salesman from out of state whose business had brought him to our small rural community. After spending the evening in a bar, he had returned to his motel room to continue drinking alone. His depression grew until it overwhelmed him. He looked for the listing of a crisis line in the local telephone directory. There was none, so he randomly picked a number. It was mine.

For the next two hours, I listened as he told me about the hopes he had for his work, the guilt he suffered over his failed marriage, and the love he felt for his daughter. He had disappointed his parents and was embarrassed to tell them about his addiction to alcohol. No longer active in his Catholic church, he felt unworthy of asking God's help. Finally, spent and becoming sober, he apologized for calling so late.

It was my turn, now. If at first I had felt this to be someone else's responsibility, I was wrong. In the Scriptures James advises, "Therefore confess your sins to one another, and pray for one another, so that you may be healed. The prayer of the righteous is powerful and effective" (James 5:16).

I said a silent prayer and admitted that I, too, had made many wrong decisions. "God has always forgiven me and been a source of strength," I told him.

Then I encouraged him to pray and seek counsel with a priest. As a mother, I assured him that a parent's love does not end because of disappointments. I urged him to maintain a close relationship with his daughter, even if they continued to live apart.

He listened and agreed that the support of others was necessary at this time in his life. He promised to contact a priest later that morning and take positive steps to get the professional help he needed to control his addiction to alcohol.

"Thanks for not hanging up on me," he concluded.

"I will remember to pray for you this week," I said.

His voice registered surprise. "I didn't think you were Catholic."

"I'm not," I admitted. "But I think my Protestant prayers will work."

He laughed then, a deep hearty laugh. "You sound so much like my mother," he said. He could give me no finer compliment.[4]

This story illuminates the truth that simply listening and sharing from the heart can be a profound expression of discipleship. Such actions do not lie beyond the reach of any of us. They require no special training. We can practice simple obedience to God's love in small, everyday ways.

The quality of being present to and for one another as Christians is not limited to individual expressions of care. It is characteristic of Jesus' disciples to act in concert as a community of believers. Here is the story of one congregation that grew spiritually by offering authentic Christian hospitality.

AUTHENTIC CHRISTIAN HOSPITALITY

Jan Hus Presbyterian Church in New York City, like many city churches, found its congregation dwindling, while at the same time the church was hosting a variety of groups during the week who appreciated the use of the building. Yet there seemed to be no link between the weekday groups and the Sunday worshipers. The sanctuary was locked during the week, and the church's session [governing board] had a representative stationed in the hallways to protect the church in case of difficulties. Then someone discovered a connection: What if the church representative's job description were to shift from protection to hospitality? Tables were set up with a welcoming host and literature about the church's worship and programs; the sanctuary was unlocked during the times of the community meetings with an invitation to enter and pray. Soon people from the weekday groups began to participate in the life of the church—and a revitalized congregation is the result today.[5]

Have you ever noticed how often the New Testament uses the phrase "one another"? Followers of Jesus are to love one another, bear with one another, forgive one another, prompt one another to good deeds, confess to one another, and pray for one another.[6]

As disciples of Jesus we belong to each other in life-giving, supportive ways. Some church leaders now call this quality of Christian community "one anothering." Take a moment to reflect on what this newly coined phrase evokes for you and where you see it happening in your personal life and in your church.

Spiritual Exercises for the Week

In class this week you were given an opportunity to try one form of daily examen. This week you might wish to experiment with a few alternate forms to see if one is more helpful to you than another. With no single right way to practice any spiritual discipline, you may find it freeing to try several patterns. When you find one that seems a good "fit," be as faithful to its practice as you can so it can bear fruit in your life.

The first exercise below represents a form of self-examination that you might practice every few years or so. It is a brief life review to help you listen for God's call in your life at this time.

1. Place yourself inwardly in God's loving presence. With the Spirit's help, reflect on your life. What do you love most deeply in life? What generates a sense of energy, passion, or commitment in you? How does this passion connect with your understanding of God's purpose for the world?

   As you reflect on these questions, see if a clearer sense of your life purpose surfaces for you. What do you think your personal mission from God might be? Write what comes to mind in your journal pages in a sentence or paragraph.

2. The version of daily examen below involves becoming more aware of the content of our consciousness, good and bad. We look back through the day's events and interactions, noticing the state of our mind and heart, to see where God has been present and where we have or have not responded to divine grace.

   - Relax your mind, closing your eyes if this helps your prayer. Remind yourself of your deepest identity as a beloved child of God.

   - Sense your desire to be aware of God's presence in the past day. Offer a simple prayer that the graces of the day will be revealed to you.

   - Don't try too hard. Just be open and receptive, "listening for what might rise from the day." Acknowledge with thanks the evidence of grace in whatever surfaces.

   - Notice then how you were present in that time. If you were unaware or unresponsive, breathe a prayer for mercy and express desire to respond differently another time. If you were aware of God in the moment, and your response was shaped by that consciousness, "smile to God with thanks."

• Repeat the last two steps, allowing various images and memories from the day to surface. When you finish, note in your journal pages observations that seem important to you.[7]

3. Here is another approach to self-examination called "Life-Centered Prayer."

   Gather the day. Identify ten or twelve major events of your day, including meals, conversations, meetings, and other activities. List them.

   Review the day. Reflect on each event without judging yourself, avoiding feelings, or making excuses. This is the actual substance of your daily life.

   Give thanks for the day. Thank God for each part of your day, for your life, and for God's presence in its midst.

   Confess your sins. Acknowledge your faults in thought, word, and deed toward God, others, yourself, and the creation.

   Seek the meaning of the events. Ask yourself, "What is God saying to me in these events? What am I being called to?" Write down what comes to mind.[8]

4. Examine the last six weeks of study, learning, and experience in Christian spiritual formation. Ask yourself these two questions:

   • For what am I most grateful? What has been most enlivening or energizing?

   • For what am I least grateful? What has drained or tired me the most?

Based on your responses, reflect on what life-giving path God seems to be drawing you toward. How does this affect your sense of God's calling to you?

Quotes for Further Reflection

Helping another reminds us that the goal of Christian growth is greater than our own warm feeling. It reminds us that God cares deeply about a whole world of people. It makes it easier to remember that what we gain from our spiritual life is more than private fulfillment. Our growth should be shared with others.

—Timothy Jones, *Finding a Spiritual Friend*

Our love for one another is a direct expression of our love for God: "those who do not love a brother or sister whom they have seen, cannot love God whom they have not seen." (1 John 4:20) One of our more persistent problems is that we do not see each other as sisters or brothers, much less love each other as such.

—Marjorie J. Thompson, *Soul Feast*

Small groups can be Christ's hands in the world, offering direct assistance to persons in need. Small groups can also become forums for discussion and action on public issues. . . .

In small groups we can find support and wisdom to identify issues and strategies. . . . We can also find hope and love when our best efforts fail. . . . In this way small groups participate in Jesus' mission to proclaim God's reign and to heal the broken places.

—Pat Floyd, *Alive Now*

Glossary of Terms in Spirituality

All quoted material in the definitions contained in the Glossary are taken from The Upper Room Dictionary of Christian Spiritual Formation, *edited by Keith Beasley-Topliffe and published by Upper Room Books.*

Breath Prayer

"A short prayer of petition or praise that develops our awareness of God's presence." Examples: "Holy Spirit, fill me." "Good Shepherd, guide my path." As a personal adaptation of the ancient Jesus Prayer (see below), breath prayer draws on the common meaning of "breath" and "spirit" in Hebrew. Christians understand that the Spirit prays in us as naturally as physical breath moves in us. The goal of this way of prayer is to "integrate interior thoughts with exterior actions."

Centering Prayer

A method of praying based on ancient traditions in the church, including the early desert fathers and mothers and the fourteenth-century prayer classic *The Cloud of Unknowing*. This way of prayer helps to clear the mind of its ordinary "chatter" so that awareness of God can be sustained. Involving twenty minutes of silence both morning and evening, the purpose of Centering Prayer is to remove obstacles to contemplation.

Contemplation

The soul's focused attention on God in deep yearning for union with God's all-encompassing love. Thomas Merton defined contemplation as "resting in God by suspending activity, withdrawing into solitude, and allowing the intensity of Christ's love to work in the soul." Merton felt sure that contemplation belongs to *all* Christians, not just to the great saints.

Discernment

The capacity to distinguish between truth and falsehood, in particular between human or demonic illusion and the prompting of the Holy Spirit. Generally, "to see, know, or understand the essence of a matter or inner nature of a person . . . by immediate and direct insight." True discernment comes as a gift of grace, but we can prepare ourselves to receive it by various methods, including prayer, listening, and inward detachment from specific results.

Examen (or Examination of Conscience/Consciousness)

"A way of examining or assessing one's life before God on a regular basis," developed by Ignatius of Loyola (founder of the Jesuit Order). This form of prayer reviews a time span from a day to a week of our lives. Examination of consciousness helps us evaluate how God has been present and how we have responded, either faithfully or unfaithfully. Examination of conscience allows us to discover areas of our lives that need God's healing, forgiveness, and restoration.

Jesus Prayer

An ancient Christian prayer combining the earliest affirmation of the church ("Jesus is Lord") with the confessional prayer of the publican in Luke 18:13 ("God, be merciful to me, a sinner!"). The most common form is: "Lord Jesus Christ, Son of God, have mercy on me, a sinner." The prayer is repeated inwardly while meditating, working, or walking. It leads over time to the integration of the whole person—the mind being "recollected" in the heart and the heart being purified in loving obedience to God.

Journaling

The practice of keeping a written record of insights, feelings, questions, and prayers as they emerge from within us. Journaling helps us discover more fully who we are, allows us to track our spiritual growth over time, and enables us to integrate life experiences with deepening faith. We can journal with scripture passages, life circumstances, nature, and dreams.

Lectio Divina

Literally "divine reading" or "sacred reading," rooted in the ancient Hebrew practice of meditating on the Word of God. It is a way of encountering scripture not so much to inform the mind as to form the heart. *Lectio* cultivates deep listening to how God speaks personally to us through the Word, allowing "that Word to shape an appropriate response in thought, prayer, and the conduct of daily life." The four classic phases of *lectio* in simple terms are these: Read, Reflect, Respond, and Rest.

Meditation

For Christians, meditation finds its roots in the ancient Hebrew practice of repeating short portions of the Torah with pauses in between. Repetition fosters a focus of attention that moves one "beyond thought to a wakeful presence to God." In a general sense, meditation means pondering the things of faith—allowing words, meanings, and images to interact with thoughts, hopes, memories, and feelings—so that God can speak a living word to your current condition.

Monasticism

An expression of the Christian life that protects and sustains the individual quest for union with God through solitude, silence, and prayer. Present in many of the world's great religious traditions, monastic life in the Christian tradition allows for both solitary hermits and monks in community. Monastic vows typically include poverty, chastity, and obedience.

Mysticism

Human religious experience relating to the mystery of God. Human words and concepts cannot adequately describe mystical experience because it touches on God's holiness and transcendence—spiritual realities beyond our comprehension. While we cannot know all there is to know of God, we can by grace experience a depth of union with God through love. This is the essence of Christian mysticism, where union with God in love is known through Jesus Christ.

Retreat

Time set apart from ordinary life for the purpose of deepening one's relationship with God. A retreat can last for several hours, several days, or even several weeks. It is generally taken in a secluded setting to facilitate silence, solitude, prayer, and reflection. A rhythm of periodic personal retreats can greatly benefit spiritual growth. Many churches and retreat centers also offer group spiritual retreats that balance personal solitude with group reflection.

Sanctification

"The act and process of being made holy . . . in imitation of and participation in God's own holiness." The New Testament stresses that our "ongoing transformation to 'Christ-likeness'" is essential to sanctification. Thus we can say with assurance that the doctrine of sanctification provides the Christian theological framework for understanding spiritual formation and for practicing spiritual disciplines (see below). The goal of sanctification is union with God.

Solitude

The common meaning is to be alone, but the spiritual meaning is oneness or unity of mind and heart. It is not necessary to be alone to experience solitude, although the quiet afforded by being alone makes it easier to experience genuine solitude. Oneness of mind and heart comes as we surrender our masks to God and listen deeply to the One who created us in the divine image. "Paradoxically, solitude actually enables us to connect to others in a far deeper way than does mere attachment to others."

Spiritual Disciplines

Basic practices of the Christian life that enable God to reshape our habits and transform us to greater Christlikeness. Disciplines are like garden tools; they can prepare the hard, rocky, weedy soil of our hearts to receive God's new life. They cannot, in themselves, guarantee healthy growth; but they make it more likely that grace can gain a firm foothold. Classic spiritual practices include prayer, fasting, charitable giving (alms), scriptural study and meditation, worship and sacrament, examination of conscience, and hospitality to strangers.

Spiritual Formation

The process of being reshaped according to the image of Christ by the gracious working of the Holy Spirit. This process is lifelong, for the Spirit carries us ever deeper into the reality of Christ. Christ reveals our true humanity to us, the image of God in human life that we too are created to bear. Our own formation in Christ is a witness to the reign of God in the midst of a deeply misshapen and broken world. Therefore spiritual formation cannot be understood apart from its relationship to the world God loves in Jesus Christ.

Spiritual Guidance

The guidance of the Holy Spirit in the lives of believers that comes in many ways. Broadly, the church offers spiritual guidance through preaching, teaching, counseling, and social witness. Spiritual guidance may also be offered within small groups committed to listening deeply to God and to one another. More specifically, spiritual guidance or direction occurs between two Christians as one seeks counsel from the other. Such counsel is not merely well-meaning advice or psychological counseling. It is the guiding counsel of the Holy Spirit sought through careful listening and prayerful attention.

Spirituality

The way we live our Christian life with integrity; the pattern of our spiritual practice that gives particular shape to a faithful living witness. Some Christians express a more inwardly focused spirituality and some a more outwardly focused spirituality, but every authentically Christian spirituality will include a balance of interior practice and visible witness in the world. Christian spirituality is inherently holistic because Jesus embodied the complete integration of physical, spiritual, mental, emotional, and relational dimensions of human life, all united in divine love.

JUST THE FAQS

(Frequently Asked Questions)

What is the spiritual journey?

It is the lifelong process of remembering my true identity in God with the help and by the grace of the divine Spirit.

What is spiritual formation?

It is the process of being shaped according to the image of Christ (God's Word of love and truth) by the gracious working of the Holy Spirit. Our reshaping according to the spiritual imprint of God's likeness is not for our personal sake only but for the salvation (healing and restoration) of the world God loves so much.

What is "spirituality"?

Spirituality is the way we live our life in the light of God's truth and love. It involves every part of our lives: our thoughts, feelings, intentions, and actions at every level.

Why are spiritual disciplines important?

They are the practices that help us remember who God is and who we really are. Through practicing the disciplines, we allow the Spirit to reshape our minds, hearts, wills, and hands to resemble more closely the tremendous, outreaching love of Christ for all people and the whole creation.

Upper Room Ministries
An Annotated Resource List

The following list contains information about books in the Companions in Christ series, books and resources that may be excerpted in *Exploring the Way*, and resources that expand on the material in this resource. As you read and share with your group, you may find some material that particularly challenges or helps you. If you wish to pursue individual reading on your own or if your small group wishes to follow up with additional resources, this list may be useful. Unless otherwise indicated, these books can be ordered online at www.upperroom.org/bookstore/ or by calling 1-800-972-0433.

THE COMPANIONS IN CHRIST SERIES

Companions in Christ: Participant's Book: A Small-Group Experience in Spiritual Formation by Stephen D. Bryant, Gerrit Scott Dawson, Adele J. Gonzalez, E. Glenn Hinson, Rueben P. Job, Marjorie J. Thompson, and Wendy M. Wright
Participants experience a deeper experience of God as they are guided through twenty-eight weeks of readings and exercises from well-known authors. The five parts of *Companions in Christ* include: Embracing the Journey (spiritual formation as a journey toward wholeness and holiness); Feeding on the Word (reading scripture in fresh ways); Deepening Our Prayer (various forms and styles of prayer); Responding to Our Call (serving God in willing obedience); and Exploring Spiritual Guidance (ways of giving and receiving spiritual guidance). Each part offers a range of spiritual practices to help sustain a lifelong ever-deepening faith journey.
#0-8358-0914-5

Companions in Christ: Leader's Guide: A Small-Group Experience in Spiritual Formation by Marjorie J. Thompson, Janice T. Grana, and Stephen D. Bryant
The Leader's Guide provides detailed outlines and material for leading each of the weekly

meetings. It also helps the leader identify and develop leadership qualities called upon when leading formational groups—qualities such as patience, trust, acceptance, and holy listening skills. The rich content brings a unique experience to each of the twenty-eight weeks. #0-8358-0915-3

Companions in Christ: The Way of Grace (Participant's Book) by John Indermark
0-8358-9878-4
Companions in Christ: The Way of Grace (Leader's Guide) by Marjorie J. Thompson and Melissa Tidwell
0-8358-9879-2
The Way of Grace will delight small-group participants who find within its pages a fresh approach to the Gospel of John. This fourth release in the Companions in Christ series invites us to travel with eight biblical characters (or groups of characters) who discover God's grace through their encounters with Jesus. The resource is more than a survey of the biblical stories. It is a transforming interaction with the events and the characters. *The Way of Grace* invites us to open our hearts to a deeper knowing of God's grace.

Companions in Christ: The Way of Blessedness (Participant's Book)
by Stephen D. Bryant and Marjorie J. Thompson
#0-8358-0992-7
Companions in Christ: The Way of Blessedness (Leader's Guide) by Stephen D. Bryant
#0-8358-0994-3
The Way of Blessedness invites small-group members to discover and live in the values and the perspectives of the kingdom of God. Each week participants explore one of the Beatitudes from the Sermon on the Mount. The nine-week journey into Matthew 5 leads us through spiritual practices that can reshape our minds and hearts to resemble Christ more fully and empower us to live with Christ's love in this world.

Companions in Christ: The Way of Forgiveness (Participant's Book)
by Marjorie J. Thompson
#0-8358-0980-3
Companions in Christ: The Way of Forgiveness (Leader's Guide) by Stephen D. Bryant and Marjorie J. Thompson
#0-8358-0981-1
The Way of Forgiveness uses scripture meditation and other spiritual practices to guide us through an eight-week exploration of the forgiven and forgiving life. Always keeping God's grace and our blessedness before us, we examine shame, guilt, and anger before turning to forgiveness and reconciliation. This is powerful, challenging material with great transforming potential. It should be used by groups already bonded in trust and care for one another.

Journal: A Companion for Your Quiet Time
Introduction by Anne Broyles
Let the fresh, clean pages of *Journal* become an open invitation for endless faith discoveries as you record your creative ideas, reflections, and questions on passages of scripture, or personal prayers. The Upper Room *Journal* provides generous space for writing, faint lines to guide your journaling, and a layflat binding that helps to create a smooth writing motion. The margins of many pages contain inspirational thoughts to encourage your time of reflection.
#0-8358-0938-2

The Faith We Sing
A handy, portable feast of contemporary songs in a wide range of styles, this hymnal supplement is available in a variety of print editions and has a CD Accompaniment Edition as well. To see the full range of *The Faith We Sing* products or to place an order visit www.cokesbury.com or call 1-800-672-1789.

BEGINNING THE JOURNEY

A Seeker's Guide to Christian Faith by Ben Campbell Johnson
This Christian primer is for those who are asking the question "How can I experience God?" *A Seeker's Guide to Christian Faith* serves as a simple introduction to the most basic understandings of the Christian faith and will help new believers (and longtime believers too) begin the journey toward knowing God. In ordinary language, free from church jargon, the guidances are organized in six overarching themes, essential to the Christian faith: Getting Your Bearings, Naming Your Hunger, Learning a New Language, Discovering the Book, Expressing the Faith, and Reaching Farther.
#0-8358-0907-2

Seeker's Guide to Christian Faith Packet (10 books + free Leader's Guide)
#0-8358-0908-0

Heart Whispers: Benedictine Wisdom for Today by Elizabeth J. Canham
Heart Whispers offers insights from Benedictine spirituality to help us realize the need for faithful living and balance in today's stressful world. Readers will discover anew that life with God is a journey that grows richer and more blessed as we respond to divine grace. Leader's Guide (0-8358-0893-9) with ten sessions available.
#0-8358-0892-0

Invitation to Presence: A Guide to Spiritual Disciplines by Wendy J. Miller
For those who find the classical disciplines in church traditions a little stuffy and inaccessible, *Invitation to Presence* provides a user-friendly approach to the world of spiritual disciplines

based on Jesus' understanding of ministry. Miller encourages us to accept Jesus' invitation to "come and see" the stumbling blocks in our way, the disciplines available to us to remove these obstacles, and the work and presence of God in our lives. Miller's book can be used by individuals or small groups; a twelve-session leader's guide (#0-8358-0774-6) is also available. #0-8358-0736-3

Journaling: A Spiritual Journey by Anne Broyles
In this revised and expanded edition of her best-selling book, Broyles offers new stories, guided meditations, and questions to help you enrich your relationship with God through spiritual writing. The book includes practical advice for journaling and sufficient space for practicing each of the six methods of journaling the author outlines. Appropriate for individuals or small groups, *Journaling* is an excellent aid for reflecting on your relationship with God and gaining insight into your unique walk of faith.
#0-8358-0866-1

The Workbook on Becoming Alive in Christ by Maxie Dunnam
This workbook presents material for daily reflection, along with material for group discussion, on the subject of the indwelling Christ as the shaping power of our lives as Christians. This seven-week small-group resource will deepen your understanding of the Christian life and what it means to mature in Christ. Dunnam believes that spiritual formation requires discipline and practiced effort to recognize, to cultivate an awareness of, and to give expression to the indwelling Christ.
#0-8358-0542-5

SHARING THE ADVENTURE

Discovering Community: A Meditation on Community in Christ by Stephen V. Doughty
Doughty kept a weekly appointment with his journal to answer the question, "Where this past week have I actually seen Christian community?" In his work with over seventy congregations, he found an abundance of times and places where he witnessed genuine community. Out of these experiences, he helps you understand what fosters Christian community and what blocks it. This resource can help to bring a renewed sense of personal calling and commitment to shared ministry for individuals and congregations.
#0-8358-0870-X

Remembering Your Story: Creating Your Own Spiritual Autobiography by Richard L. Morgan
Richard Morgan guides readers to understand and share their spiritual stories in *Remembering Your Story*. Morgan weaves insights from evangelism, Bible study, family therapy, pastoral care, gerontology, spiritual direction, and theology. He flavors his insights with illustrations from

poetry and fiction. His work guides us as individuals to discover the story of our spiritual journeys and to share those stories with others. Leader Guide (#0-8358-0964-1) available.
#0-8358-0963-3

BREAD FOR THE JOURNEY

Shaped by the Word: The Power of Scripture in Spiritual Formation, rev. ed., by M. Robert Mulholland Jr.

Shaped by the Word considers the role of scripture in spiritual formation and challenges you to move beyond informational reading to formational reading of the Bible. Mulholland demonstrates how your approach to scripture will in large measure determine its transforming effect upon your life. He examines the obstacles often faced in opening ourselves to God's living word. You will find this a helpful resource as you examine daily patterns of attentiveness to God through scripture, and you will expand your learnings about formational reading.
#0-8358-0936-6

Gathered in the Word: Praying the Scripture in Small Groups by Norvene Vest

Vest offers detailed guidelines for small groups to engage in a prayerful approach to scripture. The author presents this process in a creative way by giving instructions and then illustrating with a description of a small group that is using this approach to scripture. It is an excellent resource for groups that wish to pray the scriptures together.
#0-8358-0806-8

A Turbulent Peace: The Psalms for Our Time by Ray Waddle

Waddle helps us discover the comfort and the inspiration of the Psalms, particularly in light of the anxieties and stresses of living today. Waddle writes about each of the 150 Psalms. His meditations cause us to read each psalm for ourselves, to see these poems with new eyes, and to love them with fresh hearts.
#0-8358-9873-3

DRINK FOR OUR THIRST

Beginning Prayer by John Killinger

A basic resource for persons who are seeking to grow in their prayer life and develop a daily pattern of prayer. The book covers such subjects as attitudes that foster prayer, establishing daily prayer times, selecting a place for prayer, postures of prayer, and specific types of prayer.
#0-8358-0676-6

Creating a Life with God: The Call of Ancient Prayer Practices by Daniel Wolpert

This book offers the opportunity to learn and adopt twelve prayer practices. These prayer

practices include the general practice of peace and quiet, *lectio divina* (praying the scripture), the Jesus prayer, creativity, journaling, and more. Along with these prayer practices are historical figures to guide us. Some of these are Julian of Norwich, The Pilgrim (who prayed the Jesus Prayer), and Ignatius of Loyola. In addition to these helpful guides, Wolpert offers individuals and small groups step-by-step instructions for practicing each prayer practice.
#0-8358-9855-5

Dimensions of Prayer: Cultivating a Relationship with God by Douglas V. Steere
A classic on prayer, first published in 1962 and revised in this new edition published in 1997. Steere, in his warm and engaging style, writes about the basic issues of prayer—why we pray, what prayer is, how to pray, what prayer does to us and to our activity in the world. Tilden Edwards says that reading this book is like sitting at the feet of one the wisest spiritual leaders of the twentieth century and hearing what important things he has learned about prayer over a lifetime.
#0-8358-0971-4

The Workbook of Living Prayer by Maxie Dunnam
A six-week study on prayer. It includes material for daily readings and prayers with reflection suggestions. The tremendous popularity and widespread use of this workbook demonstrate its effectiveness in a variety of settings and attest to the essential, time-tested nature of its teachings about prayer. The author gives special attention to what we learn from Christ about the life of prayer.
#0-8358-0718-5

Responding to God: A Guide to Daily Prayer by Martha Graybeal Rowlett
This resource helps us understand prayer as a response to God's grace in our lives. This book and accompanying leader's guide contain a suggested model for daily prayer and material for ten weeks of study on the various facets of prayer. It includes chapters on our understanding of God, the forms of prayer, the difference prayer makes in the life of the believer, and why some prayers go unanswered. The leader's guide (#0-8358-0926-9) also offers suggestions on using the book for different time frames, such as six weeks, twelve weeks, or a weekend retreat.
#0-8358-0783-5

A Guide to Prayer for All Who Seek God by Rueben P. Job and Norman Shawchuck
For nearly twenty years, the beloved *Guide to Prayer* books have been sought after and used by thousands who hunger for God. Now, to the delight of many, compilers Rueben P. Job and Norman Shawchuck offer a third volume, *A Guide to Prayer for All Who Seek God*. It follows the Christian year and the lectionary readings. Each day offers guidance for an opening affirmation, prayer, and daily scripture selections. Job and Shawchuck also include spiritually grounded

explanations of the seasons of the church year to introduce each section of the book. This deluxe edition includes Bible binding, a ribbon bookmark, round corners, gold edges, and a leather-like cover in emerald green.
#0-8358-0999-4

Openings: A Daybook of Saints, Psalms, and Prayer by Larry James Peacock
Openings is a prayer book for every day of the year, especially written for people who don't think about using a daily prayer book. Peacock offers a devotional approach that encourages you to read a psalm or portion of a psalm each day and to reflect on life with God. He includes a wide variety of Christian prayer practices as well as prayers for peace, prayers of compassion, and seasonal prayers. Play and creativity, music, and physical movement in prayer are also part of the approach.
#0-8358-9850-4

Traveling the Prayer Paths of Jesus by John Indermark
In this six-week study, John Indermark invites us to walk with Jesus and to gain insights into prayer. We see that Jesus prayed at all times and in all places—for example, in the solitude of the desert and in the midst of crowds, on the mountaintop and in the garden. This beautifully written book opens us to grow in prayer.
#0-8358-9857-1

COMPANIONS ON THE WAY

Journeymen: A Spiritual Guide for Men (and for Women Who Want to Understand Them) by Kent Ira Groff
Bridging the gap between *Iron John* and the Promise Keepers, *Journeymen* encourages men to make the connection between being men and being Christian and provides a model for male spirituality by showing Christ as the true Mentor.
#0-8358-0862-9

Praying Together: Forming Prayer Ministries in Your Congregation by Martha Graybeal Rowlett
A summary of popular and effective prayer ministries used in local churches today. Twenty-one models are described including intercessory prayer chains, Taizé services, labyrinth walking, and Internet prayer, among others, to help church leaders start and develop their own prayer communities.
#0-8358-0979-X

The Workbook on Keeping Company with the Saints by Maxie Dunnam
Draw from the rich well of spiritual writing history as Dunnam guides you through the lives, teachings, and characters of William Law, Julian of Norwich, Brother Lawrence, and Teresa of

Ávila. Appropriate for individual or group use, this seven-week study contains questions for discussion, scripture, and reflection on the spiritual life.
#0-8358-0925-0

REACHING OUT IN LOVE

Yours Are the Hands of Christ: The Practice of Faith by James C. Howell
Many people are convinced that there is little observable difference in the lifestyles of Christians and non-Christians. Too often our spirituality seems invisible and mute to a hurting world. Christians long to make a difference in the world as a faithful response to the call of discipleship. *Yours Are the Hands of Christ* helps us find ways to express our faith actively in daily life and to make our commitment to Christ evident in today's world.
#0-8358-0867-X

Transforming Ventures: A Spiritual Guide for Volunteers in Mission by Jane Ives
With a strong emphasis on scripture, personal witness, and spiritual practices, this book provides for spiritual reflection and growth while people serve in short-term mission. Ives develops spiritual themes in mission and invites us to be open to God while we are away from home and when we return.
#0-8358-0910-2

Wrestling with Grace: A Spirituality for the Rough Edges of Daily Life by Robert Corin Morris
Morris encourages us to look at our first or reactive emotions—anger, frustration, sadness—in life's ordinary emergencies. Morris understands these reactive emotions as natural, and he persuades us to move beyond the reaction to cultivate a prayer of "the second breath." *Wrestling with Grace* is a "how to" manual about loving God, yourself, others, and the world around you.
#0-8358-0985-4

The Soul of Tomorrow's Church: Weaving Spiritual Practices in Ministry Together by Kent Ira Groff
Groff suggests that the soul of tomorrow's church will be restored as spiritual practices are woven throughout five ministry functions: worship, administration, education, soul care, and outreach. Every chapter teems with practical ways to weave spiritual practices of prayer, discernment, faith stories, silence, and hospitality in each one of the five specific ministry functions. *The Soul of Tomorrow's Church* brims with insights about crisis and ministry and offers practical solutions. The challenge for tomorrow's church is not to focus on new structures or programs, but to focus on ways to infuse ministry with new life.
#0-8358-0927-7

OTHER RESOURCES OF INTEREST

The Upper Room Dictionary of Christian Spiritual Formation by Keith Beasley-Topliffe
When you need practical information about spiritual formation, this book is an essential and basic source. Nearly five hundred articles cover the people, methods, and concepts associated with spiritual formation with a primary emphasis on prayer and other spiritual disciplines. #0-8358-0993-5

Alive Now
Alive Now seeks to nourish people who hunger for a sacred way of living in today's world. One of the most adaptable devotionals available, each bimonthly issue can be used as a daily devotional or simply read as a spiritual magazine. Included scripture follows both the themes presented and the church lectionary. With a mix of prayers, award-winning poetry, stories of personal experience, and contributions from well-known authors, *Alive Now* offers readers a fresh perspective on living faithfully. Also included is the "Taking it Further" segment that draws spiritual insights from books, films, and the Internet. Available as an individual subscription or group order.

Weavings: A Journal of the Christian Spiritual Life
Weavings is the award-winning journal for those who long to know God. Through thoughtful exploration of enduring spiritual life themes, *Weavings* offers trustworthy guidance on the journey to greater love for God and neighbor. *Weavings* readers have found that such guidance is enhanced when they read the journal with others through participation in small reading groups. These reading groups use *Weavings* articles as the framework for their conversation. Participants find that reading and responding to articles in the company of spiritual companions deepens their awareness of God's presence in their lives and in the world. We invite you to form a *Weavings* Reading Group and discover afresh that faithful friends are rare treasures (Ecclesiasticus 6:14). For more details on how to subscribe to *Weavings* and to download a free guide, *On Spiritual Reading*, which outlines how you might gather together a *Weavings* Reading Group, visit us at www.weavings.org. Or if you prefer, call 1-877-899-2780, ext. 7040, to request a guide.

The Upper Room Academy for Spiritual Formation
The Academy for Spiritual Formation cultivates spirituality with a balance of study and prayer, rest and exercise, solitude and relationships. The purpose of the Academy is to provide a place for committed individuals—clergy and lay— to experience God as part of an intentional Christian community. For more information, visit the Academy website at www.upperroom.org/academy, or call 1-877-899-2780, ext. 7233.

Notes

WEEK 1: BEGINNING THE JOURNEY

1. Elizabeth O'Connor, *Search for Silence* (Waco, Tex.: Word Books, 1972), 21.
2. Thomas Merton, *Contemplative Prayer* (Garden City, N.Y.: Image Books, 1971), 37.
3. This definition was developed for the Companions in Christ Training © 2004. It adapts and expands M. Robert Mulholland Jr.'s work in *Invitation to a Journey: A Road Map for Spiritual Formation* (Downers Grove, Ill.: InterVarsity Press, 1993).
4. Phyllis Tyler, "Wild West Redemption," *Alive Now* (July/August 2002): 21–22.
5. Anne Broyles, *Journaling: A Spiritual Journey* (Nashville, Tenn.: Upper Room Books, 1999), 14–15.

WEEK 2: SHARING THE ADVENTURE

1. Thomas H. Green, *When the Well Runs Dry* (Notre Dame, Ind.: Ave Maria Press, 1979), 55.
2. Ben Campbell Johnson, *Calming the Restless Spirit: A Journey toward God* (Nashville, Tenn.: Upper Room Books, 1997), 73.
3. Adapted from *Calming the Restless Spirit*, 83–89.

WEEK 3: BREAD FOR THE JOURNEY

1. Gregory the Great (540–604 CE), *Moralia in Iob, Book 1.*
2. Adapted from Stephen Bryant, *Alive Now* (July/August 1993): 28–30.
3. Dietrich Bonhoeffer, *Meditating on the Word*, ed. and trans. David McI. Gracie (Nashville, Tenn.: Upper Room, 1986), 44.
4. M. Robert Mulholland Jr., *Shaped by the Word: The Power of Scripture in Spiritual Formation*, rev. ed. (Nashville, Tenn.: Upper Room Books, 2000), 138.
5. Adapted from Richard J. Foster, *Prayer: Finding the Heart's True Home* (San Francisco: HarperSanFrancisco, 1992), 143–5.
6. Keith Beasley-Topliffe, ed., *The Upper Room Dictionary of Christian Spiritual Formation* (Nashville, Tenn.: Upper Room Books, 2003), 168.

WEEK 4: DRINK FOR THE JOURNEY

1. Marjorie J. Thompson, *Soul Feast: An Invitation to the Christian Spiritual Life* (Louisville, Ky.: Westminster John Knox Press, 1995), 31.

2. Flora Slosson Wuellner, *Prayer, Stress, and Our Inner Wounds* (Nashville, Tenn.: Upper Room Books, 1985), 18–19.

3. Janice K. Stanton, "The Gift of Silence," *Alive Now* (September/October 1998): 19.

4. Vickie Phelps, "Locked Out," *Alive Now* (September/October 1998): 16–17.

WEEK 5: COMPANIONS ON THE WAY

1. Wendy Wright, "A Conversation with Wendy Wright," *Alive Now* (January/February 1999): 11.

2. Jeffrey Arnold, "Lessons of Community," *Alive Now* (May/June 1996): 31–33.

3. Roland Rink, comp., "Song of the Barnabas Group," *Alive Now* (May/June 1996): 49.

4. Kathleen N. Hardie, "The Light of Many Candles," *Alive Now* (May/June 1996): 14.

WEEK 6: REACHING OUT IN LOVE

1. Timothy Jones, *Finding a Spiritual Friend: How Friends and Mentors Can Make Your Faith Grow* (Nashville, Tenn.: Upper Room Books, 1998), 113.

2. George MacDonald, "Love Thy Neighbour," as cited in *Unspoken Sermons* (New York: George Routledge, 1873).

3. Adapted from an unpublished work by Kathleen Flood, O. P., Nashville, Tenn., April 2000, and used by permission.

4. Vickie Elaine Legg, "A Call in the Night," *Alive Now* (March/April 1997): 49–51.

5. Kent Ira Groff, *The Soul of Tomorrow's Church: Weaving Spiritual Practices in Ministry Together* (Nashville, Tenn.: Upper Room Books, 2000), 112.

6. See Jones, *Finding a Spiritual Friend*, 109.

7. Adapted from Tilden Edwards, *Living in the Presence: Spiritual Exercises to Open Your Life to the Awareness of God* (San Francisco: HarperSanFrancisco, 1995), 84.

8. Adapted from Ben Campbell Johnson, *Invitation to Pray*, rev. ed. (Decatur, Ga.: CTS Press, 1993), 18–22.

Sources and Authors of Quotes for Further Reflection

WEEK 1: BEGINNING THE JOURNEY

Marjorie J. Thompson, *Soul Feast: An Invitation to the Christian Spiritual Life* (Louisville, Ky.: Westminster John Knox Press, 1995), 15.

Keith Beasley-Topliffe, ed., *The Upper Room Dictionary of Christian Spiritual Formation* (Nashville, Tenn.: Upper Room Books, 2003), 84.

Anne Broyles, *Journaling: A Spiritual Journey* (Nashville, Tenn.: Upper Room Books, 1999), 11.

WEEK 2: SHARING THE ADVENTURE

Thomas H. Green, *When the Well Runs Dry* (Notre Dame, Ind.: Ave Maria Press, 1979), 55.

Howard L. Rice, *Reformed Spirituality: An Introduction for Believers* (Louisville, Ky.: Westminster/John Knox Press, 1991), 186–87.

Mary Virginia Parrish, *No Stopping Place: Letters to My Grandchildren on the God I've Come to Know* (Franklin, Tenn.: Providence House Publishers, 2000), 5.

WEEK 3: BREAD FOR THE JOURNEY

Martin Buber, Lecture, 1929 (1993 Melton Bible poster; see http://learn.jtsa.edu/topics/quote/archive/030899.shtml)

Elizabeth J. Canham, *Heart Whispers: Benedictine Wisdom for Today* (Nashville, Tenn.: Upper Room Books, 1999), 30.

Richard J. Foster, *Prayer: Finding the Heart's True Home* (San Francisco: HarperSanFrancisco, 1992), 147.

WEEK 4: DRINK FOR THE JOURNEY

Thomas Green, *When the Well Runs Dry*, 54–55.

David Rensberger, "Thirsty for God," *Weavings* (July/August 2000), 20.

Marjorie J. Thompson, *Soul Feast*, 31.

WEEK 5: COMPANIONS ON THE WAY

Aelred of Rievaulx, *Spiritual Friendship* (Kalamazoo, Mich.: Cistercian Publications, 1974), 71–72.

Keith Beasley-Topliffe, ed., *The Upper Room Dictionary of Christian Spiritual Formation*, 81.

Debra Farrington, "The Hearing Heart," *Alive Now* (January/February 2003), 18–19.

WEEK 6: REACHING OUT IN LOVE

Timothy Jones, *Finding a Spiritual Friend: How Friends and Mentors Can Make Your Faith Grow* (Nashville, Tenn.: Upper Room Books, 1998), 113.

Thompson, *Soul Feast*, 127.

Pat Floyd, "Reaching Out to Make a Difference," *Alive Now* (May/June 1996): 39.

About the Author

Marjorie J. Thompson is perhaps best known as the author of *Soul Feast*, a book on Christian spiritual practice that is widely used by individuals and groups. She has also written a book on the spiritual nurture of children in the home entitled *Family: The Forming Center* (Upper Room Books, 1996). Her articles have appeared in *Weavings*, *Worship*, *The Upper Room Disciplines*, and other publications.

Marjorie serves as Director of Pathways Center for Congregational Spirituality, a program position with Upper Room Ministries. She played a central role in the development of the core resource, *Companions in Christ*, and continues as Spiritual Director to the program.

Marjorie is an ordained minister in the Presbyterian Church, USA. She holds degrees from Swarthmore College and McCormick Theological Seminary. Prior to ordination she was a Research Fellow at Yale Divinity School where she was mentored by Henri Nouwen. Marjorie and her husband, John Mogabgab, live near Nashville, Tennessee.

Journal